# 1,337 SPOT ILLUSTRATIONS
## of the Twenties and Thirties

*Edited by*

Leslie Cabarga
and
Marcie Cabarga

DOVER PUBLICATIONS, INC.
NEW YORK

# Publisher's Note

The America of the 1920s and 1930s witnessed an unprecedented flourish in the design of black-and-white spot illustrations and printing cuts. Anonymous commercial artists working for printers, department stores, agencies, magazines, newspapers and catalogs produced during those decades a vast quantity of small-space advertising art and decoration. Their work created not one—as is sometimes assumed—but a variety of styles. It also ranged greatly in sophistication, from simple silhouettes and basic line art to more detailed images. Among the subjects given most attention were fashion, women's cosmetics, household items and commercial services. The present volume seeks to represent both the diversity and the quality of such art, giving in particular a broad sampling of the pictorial humor characteristic of the era.

# Contents

Published in Canada by General Publishing Company, Ltd., 30 Lesmill Road, Don Mills, Toronto, Ontario.

*1,337 Spot Illustrations of the Twenties and Thirties* is a new work, first published by Dover Publications, Inc., in 1992.

DOVER *Pictorial Archive* SERIES

This book belongs to the Dover Pictorial Archive Series. You may use the designs and illustrations for graphics and crafts applications, free and without special permission, provided that you include no more than ten in the same publication or project. (For permission for additional use, please write to Dover Publications, Inc., 31 East 2nd Street, Mineola, N.Y. 11501.)

However, republication or reproduction of any illustration by any other graphic service, whether it be in a book or in any other design resource, is strictly prohibited.

Manufactured in the United States of America
Dover Publications, Inc., 31 East 2nd Street, Mineola, N.Y. 11501

**Library of Congress Cataloging-in-Publication Data**

1,337 spot illustrations of the twenties and thirties / edited by Leslie Cabarga and Marcie Cabarga.
     p.     cm. — (Dover pictorial archive series)
  ISBN 0-486-27232-X
    1. Commercial art—United States—Themes, motives.   I. Cabarga, Leslie, 1954–
II. Cabarga, Marcie.   III. Title: One thousand three hundred thirty-seven spot illustrations of the twenties and thirties.   IV. Series.
NC998.5.A1A16   1992
741.6′0973′09042—dc20
                                              92-9524
                                                  CIP

MARIE ANTOINETTE

FACIALS

Milrone

Start the ball rolling

Beauty Culture

Waffles at Home

BEAUTY
CULTURE

Beauty Shoppe

CYNTHIA

Love Shackles

Here's looking at you

Ride 'em Cowboy

Oh, Bill, I have a date!

Sittin' Pretty

"Darn
that
squeaky
spring!"

now, gentlemen

Men and Women 23

DON'T
TURN
YOUR
BACK
ON A
GOOD
THING

CUPID'S DREAM

IT JUST STRUCK HIM··

Rodeo

Bowl Your Cares Away

ENJOY YOURSELF

Don't Let the Baby
Play with Matches

ONE

TWO

THREE

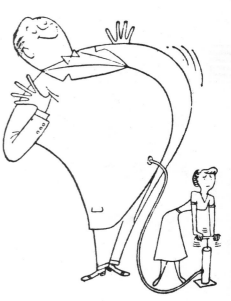

## A WHOLE CARLOAD

YOU AIN'T SEEN NOTHIN...

SAFETY FIRST TODAY
NO REGRETS TOMORROW

WAS IT OUT when you threw it?

Accidents WILL HAPPEN TO THE CARELESS WORKER

BEFORE

AFTER

For your own Safety
PLEASE DO NOT SMOKE IN BED

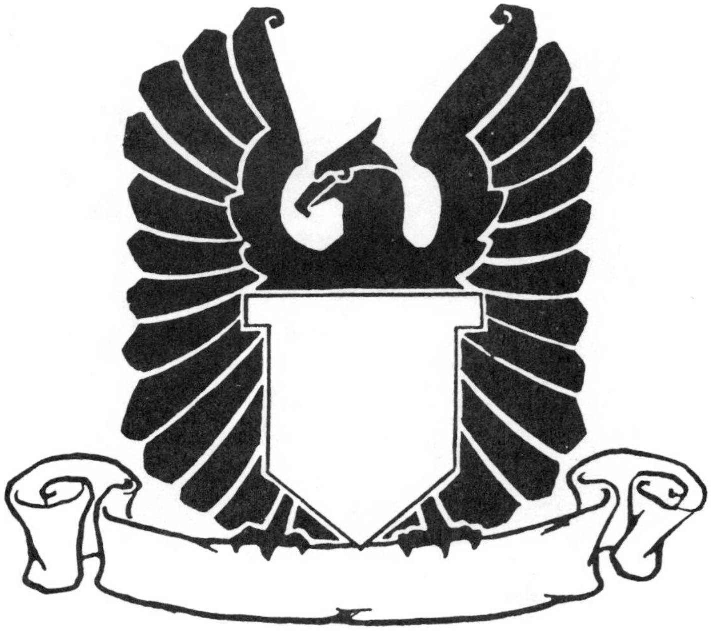
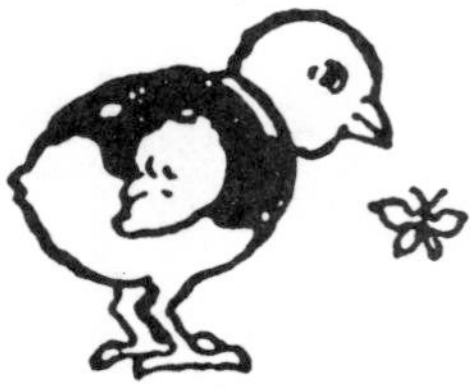
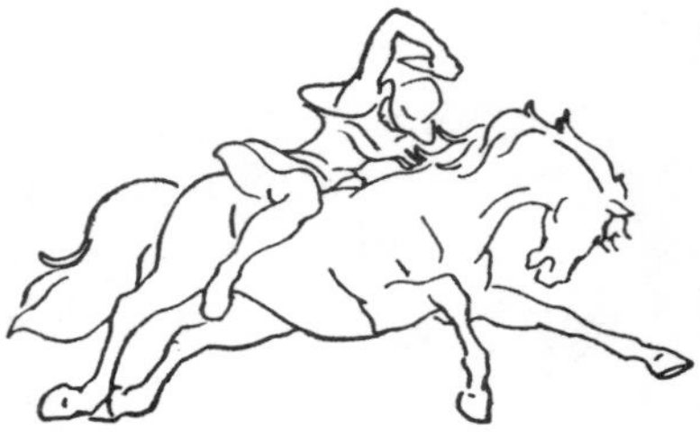
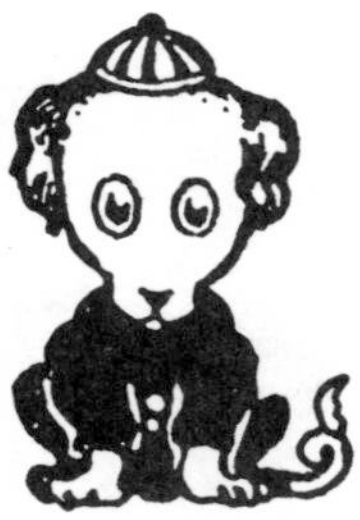
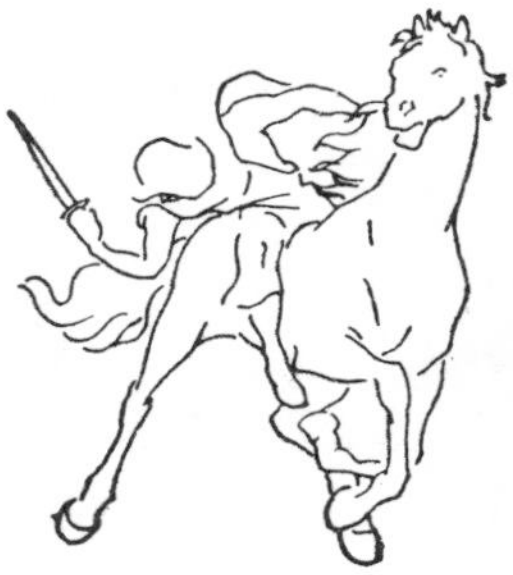
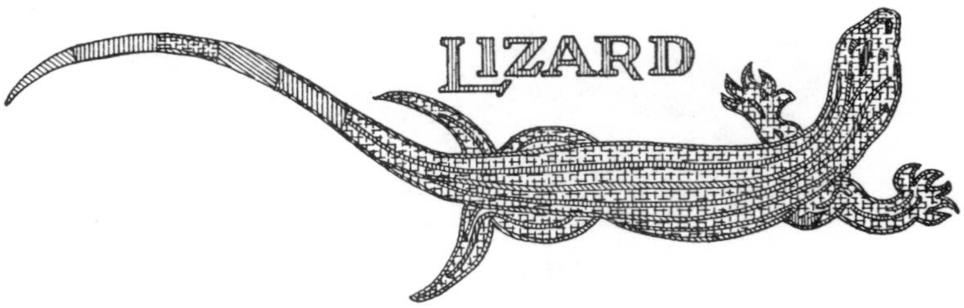
LIZARD
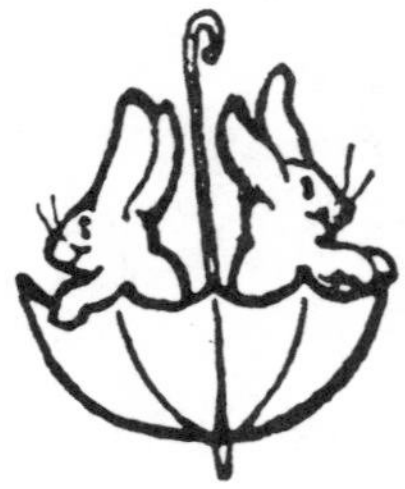
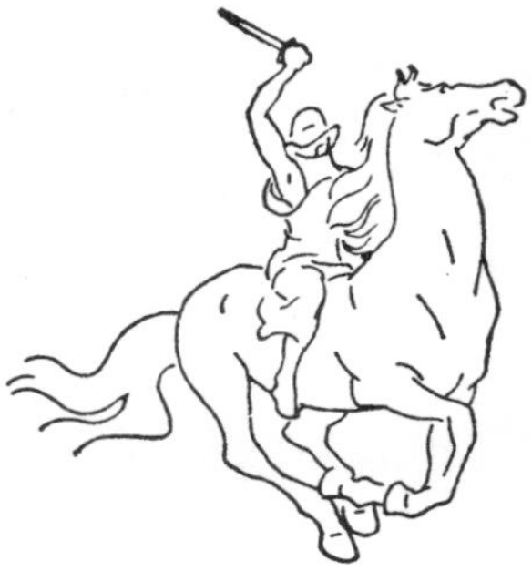
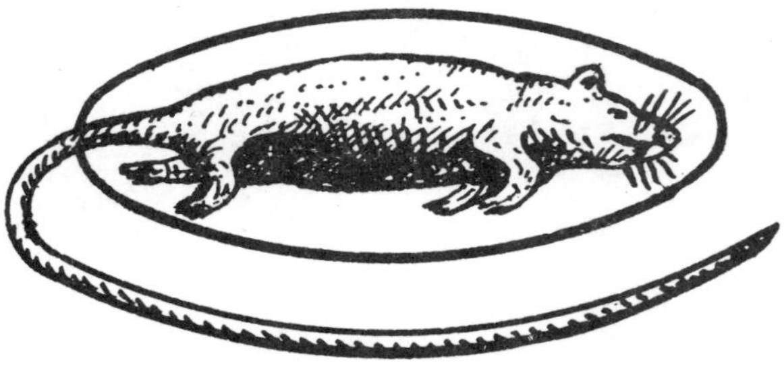
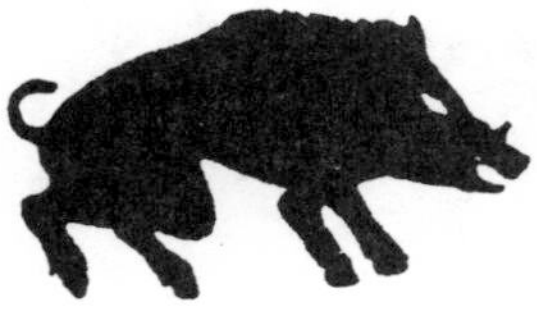
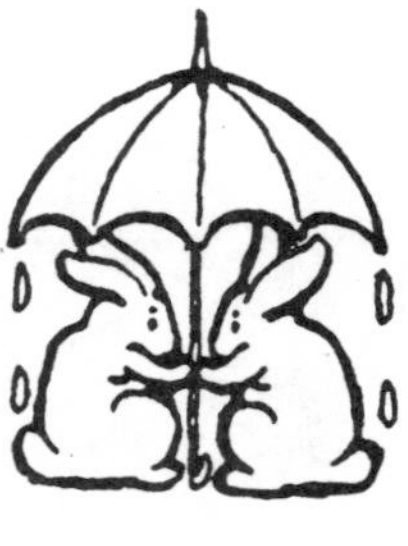
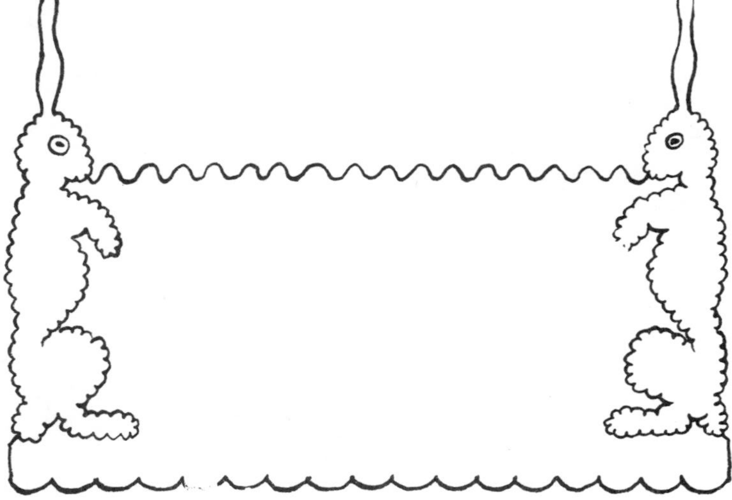
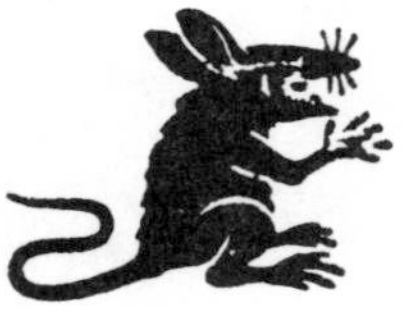
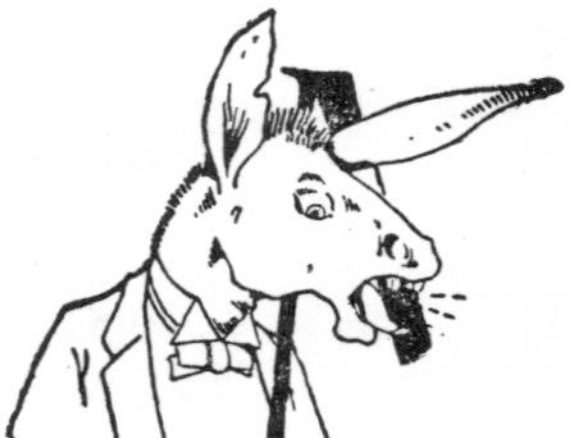

Goosco

PET SHOP

Eagles of the Air

THE BULLDOG
WITH A BITE

AD-SCULPTURE

New 1913 Catalog From
Crofts & Reed
Company Chicago

COMET